I SPOKE WITH GOD I WALKED WITH GOD

MARCHELLA BLOUNT

Copyright © 2017 Marchella Blount

All rights reserved.

No part of this book may be reproduced, stored in a retrieval system, or transmitted in any form or by any means, electronic, mechanical, photocopying, recording, scanning, or otherwise, without the prior written permission of the publisher.

ISBN: 978-0-9861335-7-2

Printed In USA

Dedication

I would like to thank the Holy Spirit for helping me write my book; for helping me remember things I wanted to forget. My family has been so supportive: my son LaDante' Elerby, my daughter Jazmyn Elerby, my mom Yuvone Raines, and my wonderful husband Jonathan Blount. My husband is my number one fan, because he believes in me, when I do not believe in myself. I love him so much for supporting me.

To: My Pastor Reverend Jackson, and his wife, Cheryl Jackson - They both have pushed me to go beyond writing plays. I am so grateful.

To: Jennifer Holmes and her husband George Holmes, I want to say thank you, because you encouraged me to believe I could go further in my writing.

To: My cousin Lashonda Mislap has supported my writing since day one - I love you for supporting me and not giving up on me.

To: My aunties, Charlotte, Glenda, and my other favorite cousin Olivia – thank you so much. I love these ladies.

I would like to thank the rest of my family and friends; there is nothing like good friends and family. I know sometimes you may not get a lot of support from your family, but when you have a bunch of family who is there for you, it outweighs the ones who are not meant to be on the path you are going.

My church family... you are awesome.

Thank you Eraina Tinnin for connecting me with Angel Barrino. Angel, I am truly honored having you publish my first book.

Foreword

I first met Marchella Blount at church. We've been there for the last seven years since 2009. I have become friends with Marchella and I love her dearly. We have shared many conversations and I have observed that she has grown stronger in her faith and dedication to God. I have observed that as people grow closer to God, they usually dedicate themselves in whatever ways they can by being inspiring to others, motivated by the Almighty and helping others grow stronger in their own way.

Marchella has become an inspiration and motivator through her writing of plays and producing them for others by presenting live performances at our church and also in the community.

The first play Marchella wrote was *I Spoke With God*. I was inspired by the performance and felt "Blessed" that I had made a friend with someone of such extraordinary talent and great love for others, and most of all her love for God. I have seen four plays written, produced and directed by Marchella Blount. They were all based upon her real life experiences that we can all identify with. One thing I have learned from these plays also because they were based on Biblical teachings is that they have shown me if I would just rely on God to help me through my struggles, they might not feel as difficult.

I look forward to reading Marchella's first book and pray that others will find themselves on a journey of transformation and grace.

Bless you, Marchella!

Cheryl H. Jackson
(Retired Teacher)

When you look back on your life, you may ask, "Is God real?" "Do angels exist?" Is there really a heaven or hell? Many times people only believe in what they see; if they don't hear from God, or see angels, people don't want to believe. My journey has allowed me to talk with God, see angels, and walk in faith. Escaping from my fears, having hospital scares and almost dying, has given me strength to move forward in full speed. You will read about my walk with the Lord and Him putting me through the test.

As a child, you learn there is a higher power. Whether your parents take you to church or not, God will make Himself real in your life. There is no running from the Lord. Calling on God, calling on Jesus, and calling on the Holy Spirit, will direct your path.

I am still learning my purpose in life.

This book is a testament of my journey and each encounter I experienced with the presence of God and how He answered my simple prayers of faith. My prayer is that your life will forever be changed, and you will be encouraged by my journey, while finding strength for your own.

Chapter One

Wow! I am sitting here thinking about my life right now. I look back on my childhood and see how much I have grown and accomplished in these 42 years. First, let me say thank you Lord. I just want to thank you for giving me life and taking care of me from the time I was brought in this world. My faith is in Jesus . . . what a powerful and wonderful Father we have in God. If not for Jesus, I would not have been close to God at such an early age.

My parents made me go to church when I was young and I thank them for that. My mom and my father both grew up in church; mom grew up in a Methodist church and dad in a Baptist church. Even though I don't remember them attending church together all the time, I knew my mom went because she took me and my brothers.

My father was in the Army and he worked all the time. Sometimes he would have to stay at work over night and I never could understand why until I was older; this was military life – overnight duty for military personnel.

I remember as we grew older my mom would have me and my two brothers attend church on base, even when she did not feel like going herself. Living on base was great because it was like being in your own world. Everyone is like a family because all of your friends do the same thing you do daily.

Growing up I really enjoyed learning about God but I don't think I grasped what I was learning at that time; I just knew there was a God . . . I knew we were supposed to pray and be thankful.

As mentioned previously, I have two brothers. My oldest brother's name is David and my younger brother's name is Joseph. We are only two years apart. My oldest brother David would go in the bathroom, take his bible and preach in the mirror . . . so I thought he would be a preacher one day. Even though I would have to use the bathroom I never wanted to disturb him because he would be in there preaching his heart out.

He was doing something for God and I never wanted to get in the way of that.

On the other hand my younger brother, Joseph, was just like me. Joseph sat quietly and watched everything for a while. Joseph was unsure about things and he would not say much unless you showed him or he saw proof... *those were the days.*

One day I remember coming from the library, and it was getting dark outside. We were still living on base and the library was not far from our house. However, I looked for my brothers because I knew it was time to go but they had already left me. I don't know if my brothers thought I was walking home with someone else but I remember no one being with me when I left.

I was ok at first but kind of scared the next.

I never walked home by myself. There was no sun in sight, it was getting dark and I started walking fast. Initially I was ok, but then something strange came over me. The street lights came on and I knew I would be in trouble. Nevertheless, I started walking faster and that is when it happened . . . I felt someone hold my hand. I can't explain it but my hand was being held, my arm was swinging and when I looked to my right no one was there.

Fear came over me and immediately I let go, running home as fast as I could. I can't explain it but I ran and did not look back. Although, I was not far from home, when I reached my door I looked back and the feeling was gone . . . I felt a sense of peace come over me. I did not know what had just happened but I knew later it was the Lord who held my hand.

I have always loved the posters and pictures of the poem *Footprints* and it reminds me of when I was walking that day and God carried me. I will never forget that moment. As I am writing to you right now I can still see myself walking and my arms swinging and realizing that God was holding my hand. I believe God made me run home to get me home safely. When I went inside I never said anything to my mom or dad about what happened because I did not want them to think I was crazy.

It really happened to me and I know God was preparing me for my journey; this is where it all begins.

Chapter Two

As my journey continues, my life began taking a turn for worse, so I thought. My mom and dad were getting a divorce and I could not do anything about it. Life was not fair, I thought. Although, I never heard them argue, except one time, I remember hearing my mom tell my dad she was not happy and I remember hearing her scream. I thought they loved each other because they never argued.

My father never liked to argue and I guess I got that from him because I hate arguing. I dislike things that are messy. Dad has always been the cool one and let us get what we wanted; in fact, I remember he gave us an allowance every other week of $20.00.

Yes . . . I remember it all so well. My dad gave me and my brothers $20.00 just to show us he loved us and we could have whatever we wanted.

Looking back, during that time I don't think they knew what they were doing but who were me and my brothers? We did not know anything about being grown and did not understand why this was happening to us. We thought we were a great family but I guess we were wrong. My mom and dad were making a mistake, in my opinion, and we as the children would have to pay for their mistakes. We did not know it then but divorces create a financial mess. We moved from the army base in Fort Story Virginia and into an apartment in Virginia Beach. *Parents sometimes don't think about the children's feelings ... only theirs.*

Virginia was wide open.

There were so many people everywhere . . . I was like "wow." I always stayed to myself. I never knew how to make friends or where to begin; and I never cared for company at my house because every time I had friends over, I felt like they came over to mess up my room. Don't ask me why, but I was the type to observe a person, instead of trying to get to know them through conversation; I was very particular about who I talked to and who I associated with. I kept to myself and just loved it that way.

Finally I met a friend, her name was Kim. I can't remember her last name but she was older and I don't think she had a lot of friends . . . yet I felt like I wanted to be her friend. There was something about Kim that made me open up to her. I believe I was around 11 or 12 years old at the time. Kim and I played outside, rode our bikes and just had fun. We walked to 7-Eleven every day for a freeze.

One day I wanted to go to the store and get some candy, so I walked to Kim's house first. I remember knocking on the door and her father answered. He said, "Kim cannot come outside she has studying to do and she is grounded." I was so disappointed. I knew how strict her father was and he was always mean to anyone who came over their house. I was really scared of him and I said, "Ok" and before I could say, "tell her I came by" he slammed the door right in my face. I remember walking away saying to myself, "he is really mean and I hope he does not hit her."

So I went to 7-Eleven on my own.

The path to 7-Eleven was straight and narrow. Usually there were so many people out walking with their children or cars coming by but on this particular night there was no one in sight. It felt strange. Then I saw a guy, he was tall and very skinny. He ran across the other side of the street and came up to me. I just kept walking because I knew the store was just up the path and in about four minutes I would be there.

His name was Johnny Palmer and he said "hey where are you going?" I tried not to talk with him and kept walking until he said, "Aren't you David's sister?" I said, "Yes, you know my brother?" Johnny said, "Yes, we go to school together."

I felt relieved that he knew my brother. However, when I asked his name and he told me Johnny Palmer, I froze. My brother always told me stories about how bad this guy was and if I ever see him to run. I never knew why but he always told me never talk to him.

As I stood there in a frozen position I said, "I have to go" and then he jumped in front of me. I asked, "What are you doing?" Johnny looked around to see if he saw anyone coming . . . I tried to back up and he picked me up over his shoulder and I started screaming. I was kicking and trying to fight but no one could hear me. Right before you get to 7-Eleven there are bushes. Johnny ran me into the bushes. I tried to grab a branch, but it was too weak and it broke off. Then I remember closing my eyes and saying, "God help me."

I was terrified. When I called on God I opened my eyes and a man was standing there. The man was a white male with long brown hair. I went to reach for the man and that is when Johnny realized someone was there too and he dropped me. The man said, "Go that way." I started running, but when I turned around the man was gone. I did not see Johnny, nor did I see the man.

The voice of the man is what made me stop, because he told me what to do and his mouth never moved. The voice was loud in my head. I really can't explain it.

I ran to the store and stayed there for a few minutes scared and shaking. I knew I had to get back. I saw someone walking back with their children and I went on the other side of the street to walk back home. All of a sudden, cars came from nowhere and people were outside like usual. I felt the man staring at me as I walked back home but I could not see him.

Once I was near home I ran inside; my brother and his friends were there and I remember crying and telling them what happened. My brother and his friends ran out to find Johnny. I was so scared. My mom called the police and the police told me how lucky I was, because they were looking for him and he was being charged for raping other women. I remember how thankful I was for the man saving my life.

Later, I learned from watching the news, that a lady was in the hospital because Johnny had broken into someone's house and raped a lady and she was beaten up badly. I remember crying saying, "That could have been me." I knew right then God loved me and that God was real in my life because when I called on him He answered in the time of need. I am not saying He did not help the lady, but during this one time He saved my life.

I will never forget that moment and I call that man my angel till this day. I have never seen him again, but I know what I saw; I don't know what Johnny saw – he could have seen something else because he dropped me, screamed and ran in the opposite direction . . . but I saw a man.

Thank you once again God for saving me.

Chapter Three

There are other things in my childhood that I don't wish to share . . . I always felt these things were meant for me and the Lord only. However, I will briefly share a few of them. Some of the challenges I dealt with make me wonder why they happened to me even though God saved me before.

I guess we all are meant to go through struggles and find a way to either deal with the pain or try to be a blessing to someone else. Funny I am saying this because I have helped others who have gone through similar situations as I have. As I sit here in tears it saddens me to know how everyone has struggles but yet our pain is not as bad as we think.

Jesus died for all of our sins and to question God on why things happened to me seems inappropriate. I love you Lord and I love your son Jesus Christ. Right now I am at a pause, because my heart is so heavy.

Do you know how hard it is to remember every detail in your life or things that have happened to you? Do you know the enemy wants you to remember the bad vision or memories all over again? Even though I struggled with sharing some of these experiences, the Holy Spirit told me not to be ashamed. It was hard at a young age dealing with someone forcing himself on me.

Yes, I was raped . . . but God brought me through a long way from my childhood to where I am now. This is only the beginning, yet I have so much to share. What I am saying is true and my journey is to help those who have gone through it or just want healing from the situation; because everyone has a story and everyone has been through things. My heart goes out to women, girls, or boys who have been raped or abused in any way.

Feeling violated and disrespected upsets everyone.

Additionally, it is hard to love people who are supportive when you are so angry and you don't know how to love or if you even feel safe with people.

The rest of my childhood was great after I got through those challenges. I really enjoyed school and acting is something I also loved. During my 8th grade year, I began acting in plays. Back stage and on stage, I learned a lot. I traveled with my school and performed at different schools. Once I was on stage it was like I was a whole different person, even though I started off being shy. I loved it. After learning how to write plays I had to direct my own play while also playing in a major role.

It was awesome.

Writing allows my hands to flow and the Holy Spirit guides me all the way, that's why I love writing. Yes, the Holy Spirit guides me and he is my best friend. The Holy Spirit leads and guides my footsteps in every aspect of my life. If I had called on him sooner than just eight years ago, I feel my life would be so much different. Later, I will talk more about the Holy Spirit because he plays a major role in my life today.

I remember sitting and listening in bible study when we would visit my grandmother Daisy (Rest her soul) in the summer time; she would send us to church. My grandmother would say, "Children need to know the Lord and grow spiritually with the Lord."

I am here to tell you . . . seek God; if you seek the Lord he will give you strength, healing, love, and support. If you have been through similar situations, you may be saying to yourself just like I did, "Why me Lord?"

Well, I can remember saying the same thing when my son was about 10 years old and he said to me, "Why not you mom?" I cried then just like I am crying now. It was a different situation that we were dealing with then but he told me those exact words. I am telling you as well. Why not you? God gave his only Son, Jesus Christ who died for us.

That is enough said right there.

"Go God," is all I can say. The Lord will use children to get his point across to us even when we don't like it.

Chapter Four

God blessed me to birth 2 beautiful children, a son and a daughter. My son LaDante' ' is 19 in college, and my daughter Jazmyn is 12 in the 7th grade. I thank God for both of them. Having children will change your life. Especially a mother's. My first born was the sweetest son God could have given a mother . . . I am so blessed to have a wonderful son.

When LaDante' was young he would read his Bible every night before bed. He learned words at a very young age; yet, LaDante' did not want to read regular books, he wanted to read the Bible. I would go check on him and he would be asleep with a Bible on his chest, lying beside him or he would hug it as if it were a pillow. I would go in his room and give him a kiss on his cheeks and there would be the bible, I would never remove it.

LaDante' was becoming very knowledgeable of the Word at a young age; I was happy about that because there was a time I almost lost my son.

Thinking back at the memories of LaDante' not being able to breathe still scares me. LaDante' was about 3 years old and I took him for a checkup. The doctor said he had allergies and was coming down with a cold. At that time I was not sure of what caused him to snore at an early age so when I took him back to the doctor (he was not getting better) he was sent to a specialist at Portsmouth Naval Hospital. The specialist said my son needed to have his tonsils removed and to schedule a date for surgery.

I was happy the medical staff determined what was wrong with him so I prepared for that day and knew he would be okay without any more breathing problems.

Well that day of his surgery, something went wrong. I brought him to the hospital but they did not have him down for surgery. I was like "What? "The doctor scheduled the surgery and you are telling me you don't have him down?" I was upset. Of course the hospital apologized, and said they will reschedule and let me know. So they rescheduled and told me it would take about two weeks.

I was so upset.

Meanwhile, my son took a turn for worse. I took him to the doctor because he had not been able to sleep and could not breathe at night, the doctor gave LaDante' a breathing treatment and said, "If he gets worse bring him back or go straight to the emergency room."

Well, I left there and went straight to King's Daughters in Norfolk Virginia, which in my opinion is, the best children's hospital in the world. As I waited for them to call me I held my son as he cried because he was so tired. I said, "Someone please hurry up." When they called me they took him right away. I remember the doctor saying, "I must do emergency surgery on him right away or he will die." I remember dropping to my knees. I knew it.

I said, "What? Oh my God."

He said, "Your son can't breathe and we can fix him."

LaDante's tonsils were swollen. *I was so upset.* I told the doctor that the hospital did not do the original surgery because they messed up the schedule. The doctor said, "Portsmouth Naval Hospital is requesting we send him over there because you have Tricare Prime and they want to do surgery now."

I really cried and said, "no way. I don't trust them." The doctor looked at me and said, "We have the best doctors working over there with the children . . . I will make a call." I then felt something so warm come over me. I knew God was with me. The ambulance had to take him so I rushed with them as my mom followed in the car.

"Oh my!" I feel like I am reliving this memory because tears are rolling down my face as I am writing this. When we pulled up there were five doctors on standby waiting for us. I had never seen anything like it before. I knew either my son was so sick he was going to die; or they were trying to save their jobs and wanted to make sure he had the best care. I was the only one allowed in his room; they tried to get me to leave I told them, "I am not going anywhere." I said, "I would not be here if you did your job right the first time."

Then a man came quickly and said please let me see him. *Omg he was my angel... Jesus, Jesus, Jesus...* he said, "I need to put this in his throat mommy it is a tube to help him breathe." He said, "It will not hurt him but he will feel better." I said, "Ok . . ." When he put in the tube my son was so tired from not being able to sleep that he fell asleep.

The doctor said, "I am from King's Daughters and I was told to come quickly." He said, "I am supposed to get off but I will stay all night in ICU with your son. I will perform surgery on him in the morning but he will be monitored all night and I will check on him." I cried and said, "I thank you." I told the other doctors to leave and not touch my son. They just stood by and watched the other doctor; he brought peace with him.

I can't explain it. I know the doctor was a family man; he was a white male with short hair and he said he heard about my story. He wanted me to know he would take care of everything and he is a strong believer in God. I knew my son was going to be okay.

I know the other doctors were trying to do their job, but I didn't want them touching LaDante'. That night I stayed in his room and everyone came up there to see him. I said, "I have him, everyone go home." My son woke up and I said, "I am here with you." LaDante' said, "Mommy, are you crying?" I said, "No honey." He said, "Why are you crying?" I said, "Mommy's just worried about you." LaDante' said, "You remember what the man said? He told you not to worry." Once again my son at the age of 3 years old, told me everything was going to be ok.

I could not sleep because I was worried about him.

The doctor came in so tired, checked on him and said, "Get some rest." The doctor slept in the hospital, he said, "The nurse will wake me if they need me but I am not far." I was so thankful for him; my son was breathing and I knew God was working things out.

The morning of the surgery we were all in the waiting room and they said, "Mommy . . . come see your son before he goes into surgery." I said, "Ok" as I walked back there my son said to me, "mommy why are you crying?" I said, "I am not crying." He said, "Yes you are." LaDante' then said, "mommy don't you see them?" I said, "See who?" LaDante' said, "The angels?" I said, "No I don't see any angels."

Then my son looked at me and said, "I will be ok." The doctor then said, "Its time." He looked at me and said, "Momma, he will be fine, I got him and just like he said the angels are with us." I broke down as they rolled him out. Once the surgery was finished they said, "He's calling for his mommy." I ran in there. They told me everything went well. They took out his tonsils and partial adenoids. The doctor said, "I told you I would not let you down."

I hugged him and thanked him, but most importantly, praised God. I knew right then God took care of my son. Then LaDante', half sleep from medicine said, "Mommy I told you I would be ok, the angels told me to tell you." After that my son never spoke of angels again.

After 3 or 4 days of LaDante' being in the hospital he was doing great. The doctors finally let us go home. This was the first time I heard God call my name. LaDante' was in his room watching Barney, I will never forget this. I was so tired I was in the room with him but I fell asleep on the floor; then woke up and went to my bed. I laid down and after sleeping for a while I woke up to the Lord calling my name. I said, "Yes" but no response. I walked around the house thinking someone was in there but it was me and my son. I went to his room he had awakened and was lying in bed watching Barney. I said, "Did you call me?" He said, "No mommy." I said, "Did you hear someone calling me?" He said, "No mommy." I said, "Maybe I was dreaming. Or was it a dream?"

No it was God, His voice is so full of power, I knew right then he called me but I just did not know why.

All I knew is that I was thankful for what He just did for my son. God brings miracles in our lives.

Chapter Five

Jazmyn... my little tinker bell.

My daughter is so much like me. Oh my, I don't know where to begin with her. All I know is that she is loved by so many. My daughter loves people, and she says she wants to be a cop one day; so I tell her that she can do whatever she sets her mind to do. I let my children know they are a child of God and he created all of us to be what we want to be . . . the best we can be.

When Jazmyn was about two years old I tried to "potty" train her. For some reason she was so lazy, she never wanted to go to the potty. Well my cousin Lauren Robinson (may the Lord rest her soul) passed away; she and my daughter were very close. I will never forget, Lauren called Jazmyn every day and sometimes twice a day. I would say, "What is she saying to a 2 year old all day on the phone?" I guess it was not meant for me to know because she never told me and my daughter would get on the phone and talk to her.

Jazmyn walked around the house and just talked on the phone. She and Lauren would be on the phone for long periods of time and I never knew when they would get off the phone.

One day my Lauren phoned and I thought she was calling to talk to Jazmyn but she called to talk to me that day. She said, "Hey." I said, "Hey." Then Lauren said, 'I have something to tell you." I said, "What is it baby?" Lauren said, "I am going to die..." I immediately starting crying saying, "don't say that... it's not funny." She said, "I have to tell you this, I am going to die."

I hung up the phone.

I don't know if the Lord was having her prepare me for this because I was hit the hardest or what. My little cousin was with me every summer. I took her everywhere. People thought she was my daughter. I was so close to her. I called my auntie, her mom and said, "Lauren said she is going to die." My aunt said, "Don't worry about it sissy she has been sick and we just need to keep praying." Lauren had Lupus.

I knew Lupus was serious because one of my friends has it, but I didn't know you could die from it. The Lord was calling her home to Him and He knew the day and time; yet, we did not.

So the calls did not come for a day or two and then she called back to ask, "May I please talk with Jazzy?" I said, "Yes." And let them talk again.

I never knew that the last time I would speak with Lauren would be her graduation day. She called me the night before inquiring if my husband (at that time) was coming in from being out on the boat for 2 weeks. Originally, I planned to go to her graduation and then fly to Texas. My husband had taken leave and there was no way we could go to NC as she was graduating that morning, which was the same time he was coming home.

I remember receiving a call from my auntie saying "Sissy, Lauren is being rushed to the hospital." I said, "What?" I could not believe what I heard. I was told by my aunt that Lauren knew it was time. She came in the living room because they were ready to go and Lauren told her mom to call 911. My aunt said, "What is wrong?" Lauren said, "Call 911."

My aunt called and when the paramedics arrived she told them not to allow her mom to ride in the ambulance with her. In my heart I believe Lauren knew it would be hard for her mom because as she was being transported (based on what I was told) she stopped breathing.

My cousin was revived but not for a long period, just long enough for her mom and dad to say goodbye. This was the most disaster I felt in my life . . . I felt like my heart dropped when I got that call she was gone. For approximately a week, regardless of what time I went to bed, I woke up at 2:39 every morning, I believe Lauren passed around this time. It was hard for me to understand and I knew I could not drive or go to NC at that time; I was so lost in thoughts and had very few words. Instead, I flew to Texas. My plan was to go visit my in laws and come back early for the funeral.

That never happened. The day of the funeral my mother-in-law tried to book me a flight to attend, but I could not get a flight out. I was going crazy . . . I said, "How will I get there?" I just fell into a depression . . . I said, "I never said my goodbyes." I knew right then there is no way I would have been able to see Lauren like that. I know that now, things happened for a reason.

The day of the funeral everyone called me. I could not talk, but that night was the best night. Awakened by a light standing in the doorway, I saw Lauren . . . she stood there and then went away. Then I had a dream and in my dream she spoke things only she and her mom would know. Lauren spoke these words to me . . . "I will be with Jazmyn always. I will always watch her, never worry about her."

When I woke up I told my husband (now ex-husband) that I saw Lauren, he said "what?" I said, "She came in last night then she was in my dream." I felt so much better, I can't explain it. I called my aunt (even though she was not taking any calls) when she knew it was me she answered quickly. I said, "Auntie I saw Lauren." I said, "She told me to tell you this and that." My Aunt said, "There is no way you would know this. Only Lauren and I would know this." I told her, "I know." I said, "She is fine and looks so beautiful and she's no longer sick." My aunt said, "I know she is with the Lord."

My cousin did what she said she was going to do; she looked out for Jazzy. Jazzy and I were at home one day and she was running around the house like she was being chased. I said, "Who are you running from silly?" She would not answer me. Then she said, "Ok I will go to potty." Jazmyn went to the bathroom and sat on her little potty and she said, "See mommy I did it." I said, "Praise God, I am proud of you." She said, "No mommy you did not do it she did." I said, "Who is she?" then she pointed at the door but I did not see anything. At that moment something came over me and then Jazzy said, "Mommy you made her go away . . . she said you were scared."

I knew right then it was Lauren.

Immediately I called my mom and my auntie. My auntie said, "Yes they are so connected." I said, "Yes they are." I have my cousin Lauren to thank for potty training Jazzy. I love her and miss her so much. She was more than a cousin she was like a daughter to me...

Rest in Peace Lauren Robinson.

Chapter Six

One day I was online; I wanted to connect more with God but I was not sure how. Just looking online I saw things about spirituality and said to myself, "I know God is real but I need a connection with Him." There was something I saw online about meditation . . . I said, "Oh my, that seems easy - I want to try this." I went into my room and I remember reading how to take deep breaths, in and out - I just needed to relax my mind. As I sat down in my room I remember closing my eyes; and then I began humming.

All of a sudden a white tiger appeared before me . . . it was so close. It had blue eyes and it frightened me. Opening my eyes immediately I said, "No I don't want to do this anymore."

It seemed so real.

It was as if I stood there looking at a person. The tiger never made a sound, it just appeared and since I did not expect that, I was scared. I said to myself, "Oh no . . . I am not going to close my eyes anymore." I thought I would see the tiger again but I did not. Meditation was not for me so I backed away from doing it.

However, the closer I tried to get to God the more things began to happen. I was in bed one night asleep and awakened by something. There was an image of something standing at the foot of my bed, but I wasn't sure what it was. I could not move, I could not talk, and I could not cry out for help . . . I was frozen with fear.

I called out the name of *Jesus* and it went away . . . that fast. Although, I can't explain to you what happened or what was there; however, I do know this - whatever it was did not want me to get close to God. Nothing or no one was going to stop me from getting close to God; I was not going to allow that. Thankfully, whatever it was did not come back.

Over the next few nights I had my first experience with an Angel. The experience left me in shock and I did not know how to tell anyone what had happened or if they would believe me; either way, I did not care. I was awakened by fog in the room but I was not in my room. Then I saw people shouting with their hands up in the air like they were cheering. I said, "Oh my, is this a rally going on or what?" Yet, I never saw the face of anyone . . . all I saw was people facing one direction.

Out of curiosity, I wanted to know what they were cheering about so I walked passed the people. However, I never turned around to see what or who they were. Suddenly I came to a stop when I saw a stage. There was a man preaching – I assumed this because he was standing and raising his hands. I never saw his face; however, on the right side of him was an angel.

I was astounded.

The angel was huge! It was sparkly bright, the wings were huge. You could not see the face of the angel but it was enormous. The angel spotted me and looked at me like I was not supposed to be there. Surprisingly, no one noticed me except the angel. The angel stood closer to the stage as if it was coming towards me and I said, "No I don't want to see this" and my eyes opened and it all vanished.

I woke up my husband (now ex-husband) and said, "I just seen an angel." I know he did not believe me, but he said, "Oh wow. I know you have a gift, but wow."

I believe right then he became scared of me.

I was getting closer to God and he was not and did not want to. However, I also called a friend and when I told my girlfriend, Rev. Mercy, she said, "I believe you." Rev. Mercy said, "You will experience things and God will show you things." I told her I am excited, but I don't understand what is going on.

"How did I get there?"

I didn't understand why I was not allowed there. Or was I allowed there and the angel knew I was coming? It seemed to me that I was too close and the angel was showing me not to move any further. All I know is I will never forget that experience.

Chapter Seven

Out of all the chapters in this book this chapter is the part of my life I wish I could erase. I moved to Texas with my husband (now ex-husband) once he was discharged from the Navy. We moved in with his parents.

We were going to buy a house but we needed to get established first. Finding jobs and getting to know the area is what we wanted to do.

My husband was blessed with a job working with oil and I was blessed working in the billing department of the local hospital. The jobs were going great, but I was not happy living with his parents because I wanted us to have our own place. We had plenty of money to move but he wanted to wait and find a house allowing us to save even more money.

His parents were nice to me and my two children, at first, but they were not saved. I told them, "I want to find a church home, and also go see Joel Osteen; I watch him so much on television and now that I am here, I can go see him." My father-in-law said, "We don't go to church around here." I said, "Excuse me . . . My children will be brought up in church." And he said, "Well not here. All churches want is money and I am not giving them any." I asked him, "Did you ever go to church?" He said, "When I was small but not now." I said, "Well my children will grow up in church."

After that the conversation went in a different direction. Even though they did not attend church, I thought it was strange that they would ask me to pray for their marriage. I would pray for them when I sat in the quiet room to read my bible. Additionally, I kept a journal of all my letters to God.

Well, one day they came in the house and said, "Hey we were in Walmart and saw this journal and thought you may want to write in it." I responded, "Well, thank you." I did not know they knew I was writing to God, unless they went through my stuff when I was at work.

The thought of them doing that made me feel like my privacy was being invaded and disappointed me at the same time. Journaling is sacred between me and the Lord – that's our time.

This time during my life was especially difficult because my husband (Tommy) was gone a lot on the oil boat and I was stuck at home with my in laws when I got off of work.

One day my husband came home from work and he said, "Hey, my parents want to meet with us."

I said, "Ok."

I went in their office downstairs and his father said, "I want to say this to you. I feel like you think God is your God and nobody else's." I said, "Excuse me! I am sorry, but how do you come to that conclusion?" "I don't even talk to you or your wife about God, unless you come to me and ask me to pray. You don't make sense." I immediately felt attacked. I started crying and then I saw a big globe in the middle of the floor that only I could see and it brought me peace. I looked at Tommy and said, "This meeting is over." I left and went upstairs.

His parents did not have anything to say.

They could not say anything once I said that. They knew they made a mistake about showing me the journal.

Tommy, ran behind me and said, "I don't know what is wrong with my parents. Let's start looking around, because this don't make sense to me." I told him they read my journal to God. My husband (at the time) knew where it was and he never touched it. He left to go out of town for three days and said, "When I get back we will move."

I said, "Great."

The next day I received a call from my aunt telling me she's been calling me and so was my grandmother but I was not getting the messages. They would talk to my father-in-law, but he would never tell me about any messages. My aunt said my grandmother was not doing well and that she wanted me to call home and try to bring the kids and maybe that will help, but it did not look good.

I was so upset I called my husband and he said, "I did not know." I said, "I will book a flight for us all and he said he was coming too. His parents were listening on the other line the entire time.

Chapter Eight

Now this is how the nightmare begins.

I told my husband's parents about my auntie and grandmother calling and they never denied that they called. All they said was, "this is your first Christmas here with us and we want you to leave after Christmas." I said, "No. we are taking a flight out of here to go see my grandmother; she is not doing well."

Then my mother-in-law said, "Why don't you and Tommy go and we keep the kids?" I said, "No." She then said, "Well you go and leave the children." I said, "No. What is the big deal?" She said, "We just want to make sure you come back." I said, "All my stuff is here; of course I am coming back." After that nothing else was said. I said, "This is a strange family and I can't wait to get out of here."

That night I went to bed, I knew my husband was coming home the next day so I wanted to make sure I got plenty of rest and besides I had to get up for work.

It was about 2:00 am; I was awakened, and the room was pitch black. All of sudden, clouds were in the room as if I was watching television up close. I said, "Oh my, what is happening?" Then, there were tall buildings, but one stood out. The building was tall and brown. The door opened as if someone opened it for me. I was going through this warehouse which was empty, but there was a chair that looked like a throne chair.

A man sat in the chair, his hair was gray and the color of his skin was not the color of our skin. It was not white or black or brown . . . it was like a peach color. I can still see it. I was amazed at what he looked like but his head was down and a light shined on him from the top as if he was being judged by God. All of a sudden there was fog again to the left of the man, and an angel appeared.

He was huge.

I could see the brightness of the angel and the wings were big and powerful. I froze, and as I got closer to the man the angel came closer and I knew I would not be able to get near the man.

Suddenly, I became fearful. I don't know what it was, but fear came over me. I said, "Lord I don't want to see anymore please." The vision was gone, but I could feel the presence of the angel in the room as if it came back with me. My goodness, it was so powerful . . . I can't explain it. I closed my eyes and I said, "Please Lord, allow me to sleep."

I went right back to sleep.

When I woke up that morning, I was so scared. I never in life felt like that. I could still feel the angel. The angel was there every move I made. I got in the shower; I could feel the angel outside the shower. It was so powerful; I could not talk even if I wanted to. When I was in the mirror the angel was there. I asked myself, "Why is it like that? "I don't know what I saw last night and why I can't talk."

I drove to work without music, I rode in silence; I knew something was wrong, but could not explain it to anyone. It felt like something bad was going to happen and I did not know how to fix it or what to do about it.

While I was at work, my husband called and said, "I just landed and we need to talk." I asked, "Are you ok?"

He said, "Yes, I am. But I don't know why you want to leave me." I asked, "What are you talking about?" He said, "I thought you were happy." I said, "Huh?"

I was lost.

I said, "Who said this?" He said, "We will talk when you get home ok?" Then I said, "Now I know something is wrong." When I arrived home, I asked my husband again, "What are you talking about?" He said, "My mom and dad said you are planning on leaving me." I said, "oh my gosh!" I went to his father and he did not say a word. I took the kids and left and went to the store crying and called my mom. I said mommy something is wrong. I said this family is crazy. My mom said, "What is going on?" I said I need to come home. I am moving back to Virginia. My mom said, "Come home . . . where is Tommy?" I told her he is at the house. I told her how they did not want me talking to auntie or grandma or even you. I said, "I feel like I'm in prison there."

My mom told me to calm down and move back home. I told her I would go back to the house so I could get my things together because I was leaving. When I got there, his mother was home and she said, "Please can I talk to you?" I said, "You are a liar, you and your husband are lying to Tommy. I never told you anything about leaving him . . . only this house."

Tommy stood there and looked at his mom and she told him she was sorry for lying. Tommy said, "What?" and stormed out of the house. I went in the sitting room with his mom. She apologized about everything and said they did not want me to go. She asked if I could wait and see my grandmother after Christmas, so that we could all have a great Christmas she planned. I was considering it until her husband came in the room.

She talked me into going after Christmas, even though I previously planned to leave before. However, his father came to me and snatched my keys out of my hands and said, "You are not going anywhere or leaving my son, and if you ever thought about it, you will leave in a body bag."

I was upset.

I said, "Give me my keys I am leaving." Tommy's mother said, "Honey . . . she agreed to stay, what are doing?" I knew right then it was him all along and not her. Tommy's father was controlling everything. I got up and he came charging at me and put me in a head lock. "Get off of me," I said . . . fighting him back. His wife got him off of me and she said, "Leave her alone please." Then Tommy's dad said, "She is not leaving here."

I ran for the phone to call 911 and when the operator said, "911" he snatched the phone, threw it on the floor and grabbed me and said, "go get my gun I am about to kill her." Tommy's mom started yelling to him for help, but he was in the garage and could not hear - the house is big and there was no way he could have heard her. My children were sleep, thank God.

He kept saying, "Get my gun now." When he grabbed me I knew he was going to kill me for real. He had me by my throat and I could not breathe . . . all I could think about was my children upstairs. I closed my eyes and said, "God help." I did not have to finish the word 'help'. My God, our God who is so powerful had the angel that was with me grab him, and he let go so fast, the father-in-law was pushed up against the wall with his arms stretched out.

His wife looked too, like "what is happening?"

She then snatched the keys out of his hands and said, "Run!" I was going to run to my husband, but all I could think about was my kids and I ran for them. I know my son remembers to this day, he thought a fire was going on; he jumped up and I grabbed Jazzy and we ran downstairs.

Tommy stood by and said, "Are you ok?"

I said, "NO" your father tried to kill me.

Tommy looked at his dad and said, "What!" Tommy said, "Are you ok?" I said, "I pray the police are on the way, but I can't find my keys." His father called the police and said, "My daughter-in-law is in my house and she won't leave." I looked at him and said, "The devil is a liar you know what just happened." And he hung up.

I ran out and two police cars pulled up. They saw me running for my life and they drew their guns on my husband thinking it was him that hurt me. I said, "no my father-in-law, he is in there." The police had them all come out, the police wanted me to go to the hospital but I refused to leave my children with them. I told the police, "I don't know anyone I just want to leave and go to a hotel and be safe for the night."

I did not even trust my husband at that point.

I told the police my purse is gone, and then Tommy told the police that he hid it. The police said, "Why would you do that to someone that wanted to leave?" The police did not want me to leave; they wanted me to stay with the kids in the house and make my father-in-law leave. I said, "No way . . . this is their house, he may try to come back and kill me tonight."

The Lord saved my life.

The police wanted me to press charges. I said, "No. I need to leave the state and never come back here." One of the police officers escorted me in to get my things and the other watched my husband and his father.

My neck was swollen and red. I did not care. I was not leaving my children with any of them. I could not trust them. I told my husband, "It's me or them." Tommy said, "But they are my parents." I told him that the bible says, "leave your mother and father and cling to your wife and you shall become one flesh." Tommy said, "I am torn between the two." I said, "Well I will decide for you . . . stay here."

I went to the hotel and I cried so badly, once I put the children to sleep. I thank God for what he did and the angel who saved my life. The fear that I felt was gone. I felt safe. I knew the man the Lord showed me was the father who God was judging. I knew I did not have to do anything else. I had already given my life to God but at that point God was my all and all. The Lord had his angels watch over me and I felt it was Archangel

Michael – because of the power. I know Tommy's parents will always remember that.

Later, my father-in-law apologized, and I had to accept his apology, because that is what God said we must do. I don't want to have hate in my heart. It was not easy at first . . . I listened to Joel Osteen talk about the power of forgiveness and was able to forgive this man.

While traveling from Texas to Fayetteville, North Carolina to see my grandmother, my son said something powerful to me. He and Jazzy were in the back seat and I thought he was sleep along with my daughter. Out loud, I said, "Lord why me?" And LaDante' said, "mommy why not you? God chose Moses and he stuttered."

I looked in the rearview mirror; cried more and said, "thank you, son." I then said, "I know that is you answering me back, Lord." I receive it. I was so proud of the Lord using my son then just like he is today; he has gotten older and more mature.

Chapter Nine

Moving to North Carolina was an adjustment; I did not like North Carolina; I only liked to visit. My grandmother needed someone here with her and I left everything to move back home. She told me, "Know that right here is your home. You are safe and no one is coming here." My grandmother showed me her shot gun that was hidden; she did not play.

Wrestling back and forth on what I wanted to do … I was able to get a job right away; it was like God was planning my life right here. Getting back into church, keeping the children in church every week is what I wanted. Making money for myself again was great, because when I left my husband, he took all the money out of the account; including my check. So, I did not have access to any money. However, I did not let that get to me; I just kept doing what I was supposed to do.

My grandmother's health was going up and down; yet, I knew if I tried to leave it would upset her. On the weekends, I would go to Virginia Beach and take her; I would cry every time coming back. My grandmother said, "Your blessing is here. It's not time to go back to Virginia, God brought you here for a reason." I knew she was right; I expected her to say this.

As months went on my grandmother's health declined greatly. When she passed away I had planned to move back to Virginia, but my job gave me a raise, and a house opened up for me right away and I said, "I guess Lord you are still showing me you are in charge." My grandmother was the sweetest grandmother and would do anything in the world for anyone. I miss her very much and I thank her for all her guidance on everything I have been doing since I've been in Fayetteville.

Being a single parent has not been easy, especially since I did not receive any child support from their father or any help from Tommy. He refused to provide any assistance, since I decided not to return to Texas.

He lost his job, his mother lost her job, and his sister lost her job; all at the same time.

I told him, "When God says vengeance is mine, this is only the beginning." Tommy called me and said, "You must be praying against us." I said, "I am not thinking about none of you guys. You need to focus on sending money." Still, he refused to help me. So, I did not worry about it. I began working for a company that did not pay the employees like we were supposed to get paid.

Growing tired of working like that, I called on God; I would pray and say "Lord, please help me find something else. You wanted me to stay in North Carolina but the job is not working out."

One night, I was sleep in bed and dreaming, but it seemed as if I was awake and dreaming; however, this was not like my other encounters with the Lord. I was actually dreaming. I am afraid of heights, and of course you know, God knows all our fears. In the dream, I was on a tall ladder. A man was going down and said, "Come on... follow me."

I said, "No I am scared."

All of a sudden God called me. He said, "Marchella?" I said "yes God?" He said, "Do you trust me?" I said, "Yes God." God said, "Then let go." I let go, and the Lord lifted me off the ladder. I went through the clouds and through the buildings.

After that God placed me back down and said, "thank you for trusting in me." I jumped up out of my bed. I said, "Dante, Jazzy I spoke to God . . ." My son jumped up and said, "Mommy that is good." I said, "no really I did . . . His voice is powerful it's like a roar of a lion." My son said, "Mom I believe you." I told my son I don't care if anyone else doesn't believe me . . . it is real.

I went to the job the next day and put in my 2 weeks' notice. I remember a friend and colleague named Anita asked me, "Where are you going?" I said, "I don't know." Anita asked, "You heard from God and you are quitting?" I said, "Yes." I had to work a full 2 weeks.

I was not sure what to do - I just trusted God.

On my last day, I went home and relaxed. I woke up and took my son and daughter to school. I said, "Lord here I am what do you want me to do now?" Then the phone rang. It was my aunt Charlotte and she said, "Marchella I don't know why I am calling you and telling you this but you need to go to Cardinal Clinic and put in for a therapeutic job working with children."

I said, "Ok auntie."

She said, "Go now and get an application and tell them I sent you." So, I got dressed and went to Cardinal Clinic. I spoke with a lady named Cheryl; she told me to go fill out this packet and bring it back once I was done. I took it home and said this is a lot. Something said, "Do it and take it back now."

I went back to Cardinal and dropped off the package. Cheryl looked over everything and said, "We just started training class but if you are still interested in class, August will be the next time we will do another class." I was kind of down because it was February but I said, "Ok." So I left and went home saying, "Why am I going through this today?" And as I was going to my door I heard the phone ringing. I ran to the phone, I said, "hello," and a woman said, "Hello may I speak with Marchella?"

I said, "This is her."

She said, "This is Chris from Cardinal Clinic. I know you just left from up here, but I looked at your resume and I see you have worked with children one on one, and have an Associates in Psychology. We want you to start class with us tonight, if you are interested." I dropped the phone and started crying. I said, "Yes, I will." Chris said, "They are already 2 months into the class, but I know you'll do fine." Chris told me that she had never done that before, but something had her call me and I know that was God.

I cried and cried and I called my auntie and told her the news... she was so happy for me. Once again God will do what he said he will do. God is a God who will never lie. God is faithful and I have not lacked anything since that day.

All of my things came back quickly from the state and I had a child right away making money. It's a blessing when you can help children who really need it; I was grateful to receive employment doing something I am passionate about, while also assisting a child who really needed nurturing and support.

Chapter Ten

How can you go from being healthy and working so hard to being sick and unable to breathe? Well the worst of the worst happened to me. I had a cold that took a turn for the worse . . . I did not know what was going on; I knew I could not breathe. Every time I went to the doctor, he would give me a breathing treatment and send me on my way. However, each time I yawned, my chest hurt and would not get better.

Until one day it worsened.

I will never forget that day. The choir had to sing and I am also on the praise team . . . we had to dance and when I finished dancing my face was so red and I was out of breath. I did not know what was going on. After church service I went straight to the urgent care –

my son was with me. When the doctor saw me he sent me for an x ray.

After the x-ray was completed, the doctor came in the room and checked my chest and said, "Marchella we are going to have to call the ambulance." I said, "Oh my . . . what is going on?" The doctor said, "Your lungs are full of fluid." I said, "What?"

The doctor said, "I have to send you in the ambulance." I told him that I was okay to drive. He said, "No you are not." I saw the worry in my son's eyes, so I stayed calm, even though I was really scared. They hooked me up to IV's, and I just did not know I was that bad. I told the doctor I had been going to my doctor and he kept giving me a breathing treatment and sending me home. This doctor said "Not today. Not on my watch."

However, the doctor would not tell me what was going on. He just said, "I need to send you ASAP." So, when I arrived at the hospital, they first told me I had congestive heart failure.

I said, "What?"

The doctor said, "Yes" and gave me information on congestive heart failure. Fear took over, and I started crying; seeing my son and my mom come in there with my daughter just made things worse. When the medical staff started putting machines on my heart, things seemed fine.

Then a specialist came in my room.

I don't know where he came from but I thank God for him today. This man saved my life.

Dr. Dave said, "I need you to do a full x-ray and when you come out of x-ray I will be there waiting for you." I was so scared, but the male nurse on duty at the time told me, "I will be with you the whole time." He was real concerned, which helped me feel comfortable; he stayed in the room with me the whole time they were running all these tests.

As soon as I came out, the specialist was waiting in hallway. He said, "I will go check and see if my pictures are up." The whole time I prayed, "Lord help me. You are the only one who can fix this." All of a sudden the specialist came in the room and said, "Your heart is great."

I said, "What?" He said, "You have double pneumonia." He then told me if I had gone to sleep that night, I would not have awakened, because both lungs were full of fluid. I cried so badly. The doctor said, "I want the fluid drained right away." I did not trust any other doctor in the hospital after that, and begged Dr. Dave, "please don't leave . . . the doctor I was seeing did not do his job." Dr. Dave said, "I am writing a report and don't ever go see him again, because your lungs did not get this full overnight."

While in the hospital, I had visitors come and see me from family and my church friends. I thank God for all of them coming; especially my mom and children. My Pastor Rev. Jackson came to visit me and pray, and when he did, he said something that helped change my life forever. On the day he came to visit me in the hospital, I kept having the urge to write. As I was talking to the Lord, I heard the Holy Spirit say, "You need to write."

So, when my Pastor came by, before he prayed with me, he said, "Marchella, do you write?" I said, "Oh my, I was just talking to God about writing." I told him I have a journal to God, but had not been writing anything else. My Pastor said, "Well, maybe it is something you should consider." I thank him for the confirmation at that time, because he helped motivate me to begin writing.

During my visit, there was a lady who kept walking the hallway. She was an older white lady and she had on a hat . . . not dressed up; she just kept walking by and waving at me. At first I said, "maybe she is waving at everyone in their rooms," but that was not the case.

She would walk down the hallway and then turn right back around; she did it at least 5 times . . . waved at me and smiled. I said, "Wow! That is nice of her to wave at me." The more she walked by, the more at peace I became. I never told anyone about this; I remember they were taking me to do tests and she came down the hallway, she stopped and waved and kept going. I never saw her anymore after that and then I was released from the hospital.

A week later the pneumonia came back . . . I was so scared; it was not as bad, but it was bad. I made an appointment with my specialist, Dr. Dave; he placed me on four antibiotics.

My body was tired.

During that time, my friend Jonathan (who is my husband now), was right by my side. Jon was my best friend and he took really good care of me. I had to be on oxygen because it was hard for me to breathe. I knew he was the one because he took great care of me and would not leave my side. I felt blessed to have a friend take such good care of me. I knew he liked me, but I never knew how much, until his actions spoke out loud.

I prayed about our relationship, because my husband is more than 10 years younger than I. At the time, I was worried about his age, instead of being happy. The more I prayed, the closer we became. He became my best friend and we started dating; after being together for 1 year, 5 months we decided to get married. Jonathan said, "I don't care about a wedding as long as we have each other."

Other than my children, my husband was all I needed. I can talk to him about anything. One thing I can say, he has been supportive of everything I've wanted to do. When I say I want to try to do this or that, he says, "Do it." When I told him I wanted to write, he said, "do it . . . I can't wait to read it." He has made sure anything that I needed, for any of the plays, was paid for and said, "honey this is your vision and I want to make sure the vision is wonderful."

To date, I have written three plays. The first play was *I Spoke to God* . . . I loved that play. There were awesome cast members who made my vision look and come alive. Just a note . . . I would love to thank every cast member who played a part in this play. There were 3 different scenes. In the first scene, I recreated the vision of God waking me up and speaking to me about me trusting in him; I actually played the part.

The next scene was about a girl who was looking for love, but she was looking for it in all the wrong directions. The third scene was about a mother who lost hope; her son was dying and she had no hope. The last scene was about a man who was homeless and lost everything.

My next play was *Angel's*. Oh . . . this play meant so much to me. For one, I was riding on my way to work and the Holy Spirit said to me, "You will write a play about angels." I said, "How will I start this play and where do I begin?" Then, I heard the Holy Spirit say, "I will lead you."

Wow! Did the Holy Spirit lead me!

My son played the part of God, there were two Angels (Archangel Michael, and Gabriel) and the devil. The play was about a girl who was torn between R&B music and Gospel. The setting was a singing competition, sort of like *American Idol*, but she chose Gospel music at the end and the devil realized he is defeated again in our music today.

My mission was to get the audience to be careful about the type of music they listen to. The enemy has found his way in people's homes and cars and we need to teach our children not to listen to everything. Not all music is good music.

The last play I wrote was titled *Mirrors,* based off the premise that we need to look at our self before judging someone else.

Writing is so relaxing to me . . . I really enjoy expressing myself through writing. I owe all of my success as a playwright, and now author to the Holy Spirit; I can't do anything without the Holy Spirit, he helps me write and he is helping me write this book. My husband is my best friend but so is the Holy Spirit.

Thank you Holy Spirit for guiding my path.

Chapter Eleven

In this final chapter, I discuss my mother, who has given me the biggest scare of all. She had stopped smoking, and three months later, found out that she had stage 4 lung cancer.

This cancer turned for the worst.

My family came together; her siblings had a big dinner and we all prayed. We all believe in the power of prayer. The Lord said if 2 or more ask in His name and agree as touching, He would be in the midst of them. Prayer is the most powerful tool ever.

With my mother going back and forth to chemo and having doctor appointments, I really took it hard. I would pray to myself . . . just me and the Lord. My mother's faith in God is why she is still here. I know there are people who have faith, but you also have to speak life over your body. You have to speak nothing but healing over your body. You have to anoint yourself and tell yourself, "I am healed in the name of Jesus" and believe it. Now, by God's grace, my mother is cancer free and has been delivered. I am so thankful to God for his blessings over my family.

Let me tell you about one last miracle ... when I had a partial hysterectomy, I was in the hospital and following surgery, my back was hurting badly. I asked the doctor for medicine, but nothing worked. I asked, "Did you guys put a table on my back?" That is how bad it felt. The doctor kept saying, "No." I said, "Well look I have to sit up." The doctor said, "No you can't. You just had major surgery and you are medicated." I said, "I just want to sit in the chair."

The hospital staff at Portsmouth Naval Hospital sent four doctors to watch me get up. They had nurses on each side of me, but they were so scared ... I kept saying, "The God I serve will see me through this." When I got up, they all were nervous. I told them, "Listen, I can't lay here; my back hurts and you are not doing anything about it." The doctors said, "We are giving you strong medicine." I said, "Well, bring me a heating pad." They advised, "We do not have one."

I was so upset and sat in the chair for about ten minutes. My mom and kids came to see me, and I was in the chair. My mom asked, "What are you doing?" I said, "My back hurts badly." My mom said, "She needs to go back in the bed."

I was out of it.

Then they left and I woke up in pain. I told the nurse I am not staying here for five days... I will be out in two; I heal quicker at home. The nurse laughed at me and I said, "She don't know the God I serve." Then a lady came in the room. She said, "I heard you are having problems with your back." I said, "Yes, I am, and this place don't even have a heating pad."

The nurse said, "I will be right back."

Now when the nurse left me, she said she was my nurse and she would be taking care of me. All of a sudden she comes right back and said, "sit up," and put a homemade heating pad on my back. In seconds, my back stopped hurting. I said, "Thank you, *Jesus*. You are awesome. I am really leaving here in two days." The lady then said, "You're welcome. If you need me, just let me know."

Not even two minutes later, this black nurse comes in my room saying, "I am your nurse this evening." I said, "Excuse me? I just seen my nurse, and she made me a homemade heating pad."

The nurse then said, "There is no way . . . I am the only nurse on this floor." I showed her my heating pad and said, "Don't move it my back don't hurt anymore." The nurse said, "I thought you were in pain?"

I said, "No." I told you guys *God is good*.

Then the nurse gave me my medicine and told me to rest, and that she was going to see who was on the floor. I never saw the other nurse again and not sure who she was, but I believe to this day that she was one of my guardian angels.

Later, I was awakened by a light that seemed to start at the bottom of my feet and work its way up my legs, up my thighs, and I said, "stop!" because I was scared. It was as if I was being scanned and did not know what was going on and it stopped. I knew right then I had to get out of this hospital.

Everyone was so nice, but I had to go.

I left out of there in two days; just like I said. They did not want to release me, but they had no choice. The doctor told me I was doing extremely well, but I had to rest, and could not do anything... I obeyed his orders.

My life so far has been extremely wonderful. Having God's grace and mercy is what we all need. The Lord is my strength. I thank everyone who has played a role in my life today; my husband, my children, my parents, my family and church friends.

One thing you must know is that we are all children of God, and we must be there for each other. We must support each other and love each other. What's for me may not be for you but that does not mean God does not have better for you. In the bible, Matthew 6: 1-6 Jesus talked about those who give, pray, and fast in order to be seen. He taught in the Sermon on the Mount to give gifts in private, to pray to your Father in private and when you fast, don't make it obvious.

We should all live by this. God is a God who loves us so dearly. We all need to continue to trust and believe, in what God is telling us to do. Jesus is the only way. I am thankful God has saved my life more than once, and that I was able to hear the voice of the Lord. There is no running from God. Either you are going to be obedient and do what he says or you may wait and it's too late.

God gives us all free will.

I am praying for people who have gone through what I have been through, and if we trust God, He will remove the hurt and pain. God will restore our faith and take away our fears.

You may not forget the things that have happened in your life. However, you will be able to move forward on your journey. Everyone's journey and every story is different; however, we are here for one another. I know some of you reading this book wonder how I know what I am supposed to be doing in life. Well, that is easy... having a relationship with the Holy Spirit is the key. My cousin Monica, gave me this book called *Good Morning Holy Spirit*. It tells you, if you are not ready to get close with the Holy Spirit, don't read it. I still have that book to this day. I recommend all my readers to purchase a copy and read it for yourself.

As mentioned before, the Holy Spirit is my best friend. Jesus told his disciples to call on him and I urge you to do the same. It's real, when you are able to hear the voice of God; it's amazing, when you are able to see Angels. And it's even more awesome when you know you are walking with the Lord.

Additionally, forgiveness will set you free. A weight gets lifted off of your chest when you forgive, I know from personal experience.

God will make the impossible possible if you just have faith; as small as a little mustard seed.

When Jesus went out looking for disciples he purposed to change the ones that needed to be changed. How can someone help someone else if they have never been through anything? How can someone tell a child to just believe in something if they are unsure about it? You must first know the Lord for yourself. When you know him then you can teach your children about him and how wonderful he is and what he did for us all.

God created us to be different; to learn from each other and to grow with each other. Sometimes just talking to someone, especially a stranger, may be the best. You never know the knowledge they may have, or they could be looking for a church home, or we could be entertaining an Angel. We have to be careful what we say to someone and how we say it, because we are all judged by our own doings.

We come in this world alone, and we go out of this world alone. Judgment day is real. I want to be able to see Jesus and hear Him tell me "well done my faithful servant."

I want to hear those words.

Tell people you love them. You want your last words to be words that are nice, pleasant and encouraging to others.

Again, thank you for reading my story and thank you for your support. Writing plays and this book is my ministry, and I love it. Find something you are talented in and pursue your dreams. I encourage you to do that. You don't have to do them all at once. Just take it day by day, and know you are a child of God; that you are favored by him. Remember… if God is for you, who can be against you? Write your visions down and make them plain. Stop making excuses and talk to God.

I pray that the angels watch over everyone and your homes. God said, "He will give Angels charge over you if you ask him."

Learn to ask your angels for guidance; they are there waiting for you to talk to them and guide them. Make Jesus your Lord and Savior today. Get saved today. Let the Lord shine upon you today. You will change for the better. Hang around people who are going places, so it will motivate you to do the same. Helping each other is keeping blessings in all of our lives. Thank you so much…

May peace be with you!

PUBLISHER/EDITOR
Angel B. Inspired Inc.
P.O. Box 49647
Greensboro, NC 27419
(704) 978-8679
www.angelbinspired.com
angelbinspired@gmail.com

INTERIOR & COVER DESIGN:
DHBonner Virtual Solutions LLC
www.dhbonner.net

www.ingramcontent.com/pod-product-compliance
Lightning Source LLC
LaVergne TN
LVHW051157080426
835508LV00021B/2675